Bringing the Life M

The LIFE Model Study Guide for Individuals and Small Groups

Rick Koepcke
Ruth Ann Koepcke
Maribeth Poole
E. James Wilder

Copyright © 2002, 2004, 2009
Sixth revision

Published by
Shepherd's House Inc.
P.O. Box 40096
Pasadena, CA 91114

Based on the book:
The Life Model: Living From the Heart Jesus Gave You
By James G. Friesen, Ph.D., E. James Wilder, Ph.D., Anne M. Bierling, M.A., Rick Koepcke, M.A., and Maribeth Poole, M.A.
Copyright 1999, 2000 by Shepherd's House Inc.

Bringing the Life Model to LIFE

By Rick Koepcke, Ruth Ann Koepcke, Maribeth Poole M.A., and E. James Wilder.
Copyright 2002, 2004, 2009

ISBN 978-0-9674357-1-8

Published by  **Shepherd's House Inc.**
P.O. Box 40096
Pasadena, CA 91114

Distributed by www.lifemodel.org

Contents

Bringing The Life Model To LIFE — 5
Introduction — 5
Use for personal study or small groups — 5
Guidelines for starting a small group — 6
Group process — 6

Chapter 1   WHOLENESS — 7
Personal study — 9
Group discussion questions — 10
Asking Someone To Pray For You — 14

Chapter 2   MATURITY — 15
Changing Motivation From Fear to Love — 15
Avoiding Fear-Bonds at Each Level of Maturity — 16
Converting Fear to Desire Based On Our Maturity Level — 17
Personal study — 19
Maturity Level — 20
Group discussion questions — 21
Essential Needs & Tasks For Maturity — 23

Chapter 3   RECOVERY — 27
Personal study — 28
A Six Step Process For Resolving Traumas — 30
Group discussion questions — 32

Chapter 4   BELONGING — 35
Personal study — 36
Group discussion questions — 38
Spiritual Adoption in the Gospel of John — 39
Community Support Checklist — 42

Chapter 5   YOUR HEART — 43
Personal study — 44
Group discussion questions — 47

Chapter 6   LIVING THE LIFE MODEL — 49
Personal study — 49
Group Discussion Questions — 50
Closing time — 54

Additional Life Model Resources — 55

Bringing The Life Model To LIFE

The LIFE Model Study Guide for Individuals and Small Groups

Introduction

In 1999, The Life Model: Living From The Heart Jesus Gave You, was written by a group of counselors at the Shepherd's House Counseling Center in Van Nuys, California. It was the result of ten years of talking, thinking, and praying about how to best minister to the very wounded people we had been seeing in counseling over the years. The truths that we discovered-- about wounds, about healing, about maturity, about God's grace and healing power—and about ourselves—were compiled. Information on how to purchase this book, the Life Model and other material written by the staff at Shepherd's House, is printed on page two of this study guide.

Since writing The Life Model: Living From the Heart Jesus Gave You, we have received some wonderful feedback from people around the country who are excited to implement the LIFE Model into their church or community. Many have called or written to say they are using it in small groups, and have asked if there was a study guide to go with it. This workbook/study guide was written in response to those requests. Our hope is that it will encourage the kinds of discussions and interactions that will make it easier for the participants to find the heart that Jesus gave them... and to implement the LIFE Model into their lives and the lives of those around them.

This study guide is clearly intended to add to the information given in the Life Model book itself. We hope that you will find yourself thinking and speaking more clearly about the issues of life itself when you have finished here.

Use for personal study or small groups

As you read through the questions in this study guide, you will notice that they are on two different levels. Some questions are designed for small group discussion, while other questions are for times of personal reflection, when you share your innermost thoughts and feelings only with God, and receive insight and direction from Him. Later, you may need to share these thoughts with your closest friend or accountability partner.

This study guide was also designed to help individuals who are going through individual counseling, prayer or pastoral care ministry. Using this guide and answering the questions in both the personal study and group discussion sections will greatly help to organize the flow of counseling times. Careful attention to the issues in these chapters will focus counseling sessions on the essential issues.

Because really meaningful group discussions flow from people who have both read and reflected on the material, we will start with personal study questions and list group discussion questions at the end of each chapter. People who are studying through this guide on their own will find the group questions very helpful. We only regret your frustration at not having anyone to discuss these thoughts with you. Every chapter has application questions. We encourage you to make these applications whether you are alone or in a group.

If you find that all of the questions seem too personal to share with anyone, it might be a good time to think about the barriers that may exist for you that are preventing intimacy with others. The hesitancy or fear you feel in thinking about sharing your responses with others could in itself be one of the most valuable things you could talk about with a close friend or even a small group. Chances are, you are not the only one in the group struggling with this level of vulnerability!

While any of the questions can be used in a small group, the specific cluster of small group discussion questions at the end of every chapter should be enough for several weeks of discussions on each chapter. We suspect that two weeks per chapter would be a good speed for a group. That would make this study guide into a twelve-week group study.

For the authors, this study has taken most of our lives so far. Our lives are not the same for what we have learned and shared here. We pray that during your study time you will also be changed. May you enjoy the adventure as well.

Guidelines for starting a small group

There are many different types of small groups: Bible studies, therapy groups, accountability and support groups, to name a few. Some general guidelines for any small group are:

- Confidentiality is important.
- Members need to feel that people will be there on a regular basis.
- Members should agree during the first meeting on goals and format for meetings.
- Size of the group should be limited to allow adequate time for sharing.

A LIFE Model small group is a combination book study/sharing group. Although you will be going through the book, Living From the Heart Jesus Gave You, it will not be an academic discussion group. The truths contained in the LIFE Model small group is to help each person experience what it means to know and live from their hearts, within a safe nurturing fellowship of other believers. For those goals to be achieved, the following guidelines are recommended:

- Group members should be able to commit to a minimum of three months.
- For the sake of continuity and community building, groups should meet once a week, for at least an hour, preferably 90 minutes.
- Because of the intimate sharing that will occur as you go through the workbook, a 'closed' format works best. (That means, once the group has become established, new members cannot be added to the group.)
- Confidentiality is extremely important and should be a commitment of each group member.
- Group members may be called upon to pray for each other or be supportive of each other outside of regular group times, and may want to consider making that part of their commitment to the group.
- Suggested size of the group is between six to eight members.
- A diversity of age and stages of family life will enrich the group experience and help group members experience a more realistic sense of 'community'.

Group process

Previous small group experience has indicated that the following suggestions are helpful.

- If there is a group leader, the leader should have faced his or her own life with the LIFE Model concepts in order to lead effectively.
- At the beginning of each week, discuss how the last week's lesson was applicable.
- Encourage group members to interact outside the group to increase bonding.

Chapter 1   WHOLENESS

Way up in the right hemisphere of every human brain is a command center that develops during the first 24 months after conception. This control center will run our lives and bodies, and provided we develop a strong one, will see us through at the tempests of life. With it we can regulate our emotions, act like ourselves, and stay synchronized inside and out.

> **The Command Center**
> - Always in charge of the brain
> - At the top of the command hierarchy
> - Shuts down the rest of the brain under high levels of stress and runs the brain until the distress is past
> - It is located in the right hemisphere
> - It is a four level command center
> - Develops during the first 24 months of life

The control center itself is a four-layered affair. On the third level, the heart of the control center, we find major synchronization systems, known by such names as the cingulate, the mental banana, and mother core. It is called the mother core because with it we learn to synchronize our joy and peace with our mother's mind. With this center we are able to stay synchronized to one other, and only one other, mind. As we mature we develop the capacity to stay synchronized through higher and higher levels of emotion and distress.

Suppose that this center were to be taught to synchronize with Jesus and what He is doing at any moment? Further, suppose that we developed the strength to stay synchronized no matter the level of our joy or suffering. Could we have been designed for that?

1. What is wholeness?

2. If you ever saw wholeness in someone's life, what did it look like?

3. When it comes to healing and recovery in people's lives, what is the difference between God's part and our part? (Life Model page 13 in the green version)

4. What happens when we try to take on God's part in the process?

5. What happens when we wait for God to do our part?

> **God created us with minds that automatically seek to be whole, and the quest for wholeness is wonderfully boosted by joy.**
> *Life Model* page 22

6. Redemption comes when God touches our wounds, illusions and distorted development. How would you describe the way redemption works?

7. How is being redeemed different than being rescued?

8. How does redemption fit in with the biblical concept that "All things have become new" which some Christians cite to argue that we don't need to deal with the past as believers? In other words, why can we not always leave the past in the past?

9. Can you put into your own words the difference between joy and happiness?

10. What kind of healing do we need from these two types of trauma?
    - Type A-

    - Type B-

11. What might redemption look like in each type of trauma?
    - Type A-

    - Type B-

Personal study

1. When have you seen God's redemption being played out in your life? (Life Model pp.15-16 in the green version.)

2. When have you attempted to take over God's part in redemption so you could make things turn out right?

3. When have you expected God to take over your human responsibility, either in your own life or the life of someone else?

4. What was the result?

5. What is an example of a Type A trauma that occurred in your life?

6. What is an example of a Type B trauma that occurred in your life?

7. What is the difference in the effects that these two kinds of trauma have had on you?

8. What have you learned about God that keeps you from reaching out for healing?

9. What can you imagine God's redemption could look like in your life?

10. Who could you let in to your life to pray with you for wholeness?

Group discussion questions

1. There are several essential components to individual wholeness listed in Chapter 1. Which concept do you presently desire to experience more of and why?

> **Wholeness**
> - **Belonging**
> - **Receiving and giving life**
> - **Recovery from trauma**
> - **Maturity**
> - **Learning to know our hearts**

2. Which concept is the hardest for you to understand?

3. What do you think it means to experience 'belonging', and when have you experienced it?

4. One way to define 'wholeness' is that we are able to be ourselves at all times, in all situations. When do you find yourself in a role that inhibits you from being authentic?

5. God put His characteristics in your heart. What aspects of your true self would you like people to experience more often?

6. What would it be like for you to 'be yourself' in all situations?

7. 'Community' can be defined as the group identity where the characteristics of our hearts are nurtured and affirmed. What comprised your 'community' when you were growing up (people, places, structures)?

8. Were you nurtured and affirmed in ways that reached your soul and heart?

9. How were you not nurtured and affirmed as you grew up?

10. How different were your growing up years from what you experience today?

11. With whom have you found the most meaningful sense of belonging as an adult?

12. Can you recount a time when you were not happy but experienced joy?

13. Bring a photograph to group that represents joy to you.

14. What gets in the way of you experiencing joy?

15. How can we give joy to each other?
    a. in our families?

    b. in our small group?

    c. in our church?

16. How can we help each other learn how to return to joy?

17. Who helps you return to joy?

18. Who would you like to help return to joy?

19. Part of our brokenness stems from trauma—both "Type A" and "Type B". Discuss with the group what it means to suffer these different types of trauma.

20. Reaching out for healing can be difficult. What views of God have you heard that may restrict how people reach out for the healing they need?

21. Are there five people you could let in on your needs, so they could help you pray? We suggest that everyone in the group, as well as individuals seeking a transformation in their lives, ask five friends to pray for them during the process. List five people who could pray for you while you finish this study.

    1. _____
    2. _____
    3. _____
    4. _____
    5. _____

    Give them each a copy of the *Asking Someone to Pray for You* guidelines.

Asking Someone To Pray For You

Anyone undertaking the difficult and courageous task of healing their soul and personality needs to be supported by at least five people who pray regularly for them. You will need to develop such a network if you don't have one already. These people will be like a spiritual 'blood supply' to help meet your recovery needs.

Many of us have never asked anyone to pray for us, beyond an occasional prayer request. Most people will say they do not know how to pray for someone when they are asked. This list will help guide you as you discuss with them how they can pray for you. As you grow, you will also learn to pray for others. You can also use this guide to tell others how you will be praying for them.

1. Pray for my maturity. Help me reach maturity in all areas of my life:
   Spiritual, emotional, physical, intellectual, relational, financial.
   A. In order to become mature, people must be willing to do hard work. Pray that I will be encouraged to work hard, and that you will know how to encourage me.
   B. Growing mature means that my needs are being met. I will keep you informed each week on what my current needs are as I discover them. Together we will ask and give thanks as those needs are met.
   C. Maturity only develops in committed relationships. Pray that I receive the necessary, divinely appointed relationships in which I can receive and give life. Pray for spiritual mothers, fathers, brothers, and sisters to adopt me into the spiritual family. Pray that I will be open to these adoptions.

2. Pray for my redemption. Redemption's work must spread to my body, soul, mind, spirit, relationships, and history, until every way in which the enemy of our souls has injured me has been redeemed. This redemption would include my SALVATION and deliverance from evil, healing and restoration to full fellowship with God and His people.
   A. Pray for my protection from evil. Pray that I will be delivered from all power, dominion and effects of evil in my life and my history. Pray that this work be completed both within and around me. Pray that I will be guided to those believers who are gifted in helping me win this battle.
   B. Pray for the healing of my spirit, mind, soul and body.
   C. Pray for the restoration of full fellowship to God and the people He has given me for my spiritual family.
   D. Pray for God's timing in all of these ministries. Pray that He will reveal to you, to me and to those ministering when each type of ministry should be sought.

3. Pray for my equipping. Pray also for the equipping of my counselors, pastors and spiritual family. Specifically ask God what He has given you to equip me so that I will be prepared when I enter my prayer, healing, deliverance and counseling sessions. Help insure that I am ready for the challenge ahead.

4. Join me in praise and thanksgiving after each gift from God. Let us take joy together for what God does. Help me to remember to celebrate and live fully the LIFE God is giving to me.

Permission granted to copy this page.

Chapter 2   MATURITY

1. What is maturity?

> **Maturity is not a spiritual gift nor is it a by-product of salvation. It is something we as Christians must work on our entire lives.**
> *Life Model* page 13

2. Does added maturity give people added value?

3. What are the differences between maturing and healing?

Before we can go anywhere with maturing however, we must deal with its greatest obstacle—fear. Fear looks at question two (about maturity and value) and asks, "Is there something wrong with me?" and "What will happen if people find out?" Love and desire, on the other hand, look at the same issue and say, "Give me some of that maturity!"

In fact, the identity center at the front of the brain is fueled by desire and love. The fear centers in the back of the brain, however, try to find their way out of problems. In order to mature we must face problems, take on problems, overcome problems, fail frequently and keep going because we want to—we love to be ourselves and grow.

> **Front and Back of the Brain**
> **Front**
> - Desire
> - Identity
> - Personal preference
>
> **Back**
> - Fear
> - Avoidance
> - Problem solving
>
> *Brain activity shifts from back to front after trauma resolution.*

Because we must first deal with love and fear bonds (which provide our motivation through either love or fear and send us either to the front or back of our brains accordingly) we have divided this study into two sections: first—love versus fear, and second—maturity levels. Both the personal study section and the group discussion section are divided this way. It would make sense for a study group to do the love and fear sections one week and the maturity sections the next.

Changing Motivation From Fear to Love

Our direction and goals come from our thoughts. Our motivation comes from our emotions. While we work very hard to educate our thoughts and correct our beliefs, few people train or perfect their motivation with equal discipline. As far as our nervous systems are concerned, our minds run well when motivated by love and desire and poorly when motivated by fear. From a moral point of view, love is also superior. Perfect, that is to say, mature teleios love casts out fear. (1 John 4:18)

It should not come as a surprise that fear motives creep into our lives as we fail to mature properly. We learn our motivation during infancy through bonded relationships. Whatever emotions our parents use to motivate us become our internal source of motivation during life. If these early bonds form from love and closeness they serve us well but if they form from fear and the avoidance of pain our motivational system stays immature.

Fear bonds form as the result of failed attempts at self-preservation. While self-preservation is the great value of fear, early experiences in fearful relationships we cannot escape produce very negative and upsetting internal emotions. When these unpleasant emotions exceed our capacity to return to joy and quiet on our own, we begin to avoid pain as a form of self-preservation. After a while, avoiding pain becomes the central focus of fear bonds even when there is no real risk of overwhelming our capacity.

Once avoiding pain becomes the goal we hear phrases like, "What if he gets mad?" "Are you going to be upset?" "I'm afraid that—fill in the blank" "I'd be too embarrassed!" "You are such a jerk!" "I have to make him/it stop." I can't stand it when…" "What difference will it make?"

We must then ask a serious question about avoiding pain and overwhelming feelings. Is it self-preservation if I stop being and acting like myself? When I no longer do or say or act like what I really feel inside isn't my "self" lost? When I can no longer even figure out what I want, feel or even think, haven't I lost my "self" already?

What we discover in many people who are fear-bonded and fear-motivated is a loss and obscuring of personal feelings, thoughts, values and desires. They are afraid to make an impact on others. Often the fear is that they will not have an impact or make a difference. Fear bonded people are also quite confused about what fears are theirs and which ones belong to others. Just being around anxious people makes them edgy or distressed. They often withdraw, placate, entertain or please others to make the fear stop. Often the result is that they take on responsibilities that are not theirs because they are afraid of what will happen if they don't. Other times they shrink back from their duties because they feel inadequate.

Another group of fear-bonded individuals are afraid to let others have an impact because they fear losing their own impact. These controllers frequently control people around them with anger, contempt, rejection, ridicule, the "silent treatment," and other ways of creating pain, including physical violence.

Naturally we recognize these behaviors as representing brains that have lost their synchronization at level 2. They are operating out of fear and a desire to make things stop instead of synchronizing with others (level 3) or expressing their own values, goals, desires and preferences (level 4.) They have lost their flavor. They have ceased to be lights. Thinking they are preserving themselves they have lost themselves and disappeared.

Before we can understand how to change a fear-bond back to a desire/love-bond, let us review how a healthy identity would deal with fears at each level of development. From this review we can see where we need to start correcting the fear-bond.

Avoiding Fear-Bonds at Each Level of Maturity

1. **Infant maturity**
    a. Recognize the fear (what am I really afraid of?)
    b. Know who I want with me when I am afraid
    c. Discover what I want (desire)
    d. Talk about my fear

2. **Child Maturity**
    a. Recognize my part in the fearful situation
    b. Recognize the other person's part in the fearful situation
    c. Use a third person to check my reality
    d. Separate my responsibility from yours (a+b)
    e. Learn to be myself rather than control others

3. **Adult**
    a. Stay in relationship while letting others have fears
    b. Do nothing about what others fear-let them handle it
    c. Take care of our own business with personal style
    d. Remind self and others about our mutual goals and desires

There is a big separation between adult and higher levels of maturity when it comes to handling fears. Up to this point every person is responsible for their own fears and no one else's. Without many years of practice distinguishing this fear is mine from that fear is yours, then moving to higher levels of dealing with fear will only bring confusion about responsibility. The shift of responsibility from dealing with my own fears to helping others with their fears is a major sign of dysfunction when it is attempted by anyone of adult maturity or lower. Even for parents, taking on the fears of others is dysfunctional outside the parent/child relationship.

Parents must be very careful not to develop fear-bonds in their children. Since parents want to build capacity in their children, they help children back to joy from fear and teach them to act like themselves during manageable levels of the emotion.

4. **Parent**
    a. Help one's personal people (natural and spiritual family)
    b. Take some shared responsibility for the fears of younger minds
    c. Identify fears in younger mind
    d. Help younger mind return to joy and peace

5. **Elder**
    a. Help "at risk," isolated, marginalized people
    b. Identify community fears
    c. Help community remember what is like us to do
    d. Remain a non-anxious presence

Elders, as we know, act like parents-at-large for their communities. Elders will provide just barely enough security for people to recognize and face their own fears knowing that they are not alone and remembering what is really important to "our people" under these scary conditions.

Converting Fear to Desire Based On Our Maturity Level

Now, the reason for our discussion was to change fear-bonds to love-bonds where our desires and identity can shine. To make a change from fear to love we start first with the adult level. If we can correct the problem at this level it will be easiest. The adult will simply think and decide differently and the problem is solved.

Solutions:

1. Confidently be yourself. Take care of your business. Stay in relationship with others around you who are anxious but do nothing about their part of the problem. Speak of mutual goals that are important during this time of threat and fear.

If this adult solution worked, then you have corrected the fear bond. This does not mean that others will not react by trying to put pressure on you to become frightened again, so you may have to make this correction several times under even more pressure and anxiety from others.

If you still feel fear or cannot imagine how to use an adult solution we must go deeper and correct some earlier problems that lead to fear bonds. First we look at the child level skills. Resolving fear-bonds at the child level is not just a matter of understanding and choosing differently. These solutions take longer and involve study and consultation with others. They require a good deal of problem solving to figure out "mine" from "yours." We generally do not solve these problems without consultation and encouragement.

2. Define your responsibilities carefully. Go through the demands you feel you must meet and see which ones are logically yours and which are unreasonable. Find someone qualified to double-check your judgment. Now, be equally clear when you are trying to solve someone else's problem or fear. You should now be able to speak clearly about what is yours and what is someone else's part of the problem and solution.
3. Check to see if someone else is controlling you by being upset or threatening to become upset. If you are being controlled return to step 2 until you can speak calmly and clearly to them about your responsibilities and boundaries.
4. Check and see if you are attempting to control others through your threats or upset. If so return to step 2 until you can speak calmly and clearly to them about your responsibilities and boundaries.

If you still fear and cannot imagine or manage to speak clearly to others about your responsibilities and limits, then we must go deeper and correct problems and develop skills needed for the infant level. We get here when we can't figure things out on our own or even if we do, the fear is strong enough that we can't talk freely and openly about who we are so our "self" continues to be hidden and lost when we are afraid.

5. Find out what I am really afraid of with help from experienced minds. Often what I am afraid of is not a current day reality or what it seems to me. I may think I am afraid I am not doing my job but I am really afraid someone will be angry or ridicule me. I am afraid I will not survive being ridiculed because of my early life experiences.
6. I must discover who I want with me when I am afraid and what I want them to do with or for me. I need someone who can handle the fear without being overwhelmed and help me focus on myself instead of the threat I perceive.
7. I must discover what I really want and what really matters most to me in the current situation so that I can express my goals and values.
8. I must learn to speak about what matters to me even while I feel afraid by having someone patiently help me find words I can mean and practice saying them in a low threat situation until I am ready to speak of my values, goals and preferences to others who are afraid or of whom I am afraid.

This process of defining and expressing our identities gets much easier as our identities mature and become solid. The farther we have grown, the easier it is to change fear-bonds to love-bonds.

Personal study

Love bonds and fear bonds

When fears are shared because both people fear the same thing, their interaction begins to be based on avoiding what they fear.

> **Examples of Fear Bonds**
> - Fear of losing a relationship
> - Fear of not being understood, minimized, misjudged, condemned
> - Fear of other's disapproval
> - Fear of the other's anger

1. What are some of the present-day fears you have in your current relationships?

> **Steps For Changing Fear Bonds To Love Bonds**
> 1. Know and enjoy who you are.
> 2. Take responsibility for your own actions and feelings.
> 3. Recognize fear bonds in present relationships and interactions.
> 4. Let go of trying to control results.
> *Life Model* pages 32-33

2. What are some personal character traits in you that reflect our God and give you a deep sense of satisfaction?

3. How can you live out of these qualities rather than the specific fears that sabotage your intimate relationships?

4. Can you describe a way in which you become more focused on outcomes or changes you want to see in another person rather than your own actions and reactions?

5. How would you be different if you focused more on living out of the Christ-like qualities in you rather than your urgency to change another person or situation?

6. What scares you in this envisioned scenario?

Maturity Level

It is important to be able to look at the different levels of maturity without assigning value to them. In other words, identifying yourself or others at a level of maturity is not a negative judgment, but simply a description of your present maturity level.

Study the maturity charts at the end of this chapter of the study guide to answer the following questions.

1. What stage are you in your maturity?

2. What would be your ideal maturity level right now?

3. Where is your maturity level when you are upset?

4. Which stage (based on the maturity indicators) sounds like the stage where you have spent much of your life?

5. Which maturity indicators support your conclusion?

6. Since we cannot skip stages, what stage is next in line for you?

7. What unmet needs or tasks keep you from moving to your next level of maturity?

8. Do you have a community around you that will undertake the community tasks you need?

9. What specific tasks should you work on next to do your part?

10. If you are a parent, what aspects of joyful maturity do you plan to improve in your children?

Group discussion questions

Love bonds and fear bonds

1. When have you experienced love bonds and what did they feel like?

2. When have you experienced fear bonds and what did they feel like?

3. Have you ever been taught to think about God in ways that made you relate to God out of fear and develop fear bonds with Him?

4. How could fear bonding with God contribute to an inaccurate perception of God and Scripture?

Maturity Level

1. What have you used as a gauge to measure maturity in yourself or others?

2. The LIFE Model describes six stages of maturity together with their needs and characteristics. How are those stages different from what you have been taught to think about maturity?

3. When can you remember being in a 'transformation cycle' between one maturity level and the next?

4. Since we must lose a lesser identity to gain a larger one, transformation always involves loss. What is the cost to go from one stage of maturity to another and how does it feel?

5. The Life Model lists three suggestions for getting "unstuck" in the maturity process. Which of these sound most difficult for you to undertake?

6. Who could help you with them?

7. Very commonly, parents who read the Life Model say, "I wish I had known" about some aspect of maturity. Now you can invest in future generations. Who needs to know what you have just learned?

Essential Needs & Tasks For Maturity

NOTE: Each stage builds on the previous stage: therefore each stage includes the needs and tasks of the previous stage. The 'ideal age' is the earliest age at which new tasks can be attempted. The end of that stage expects some degree of mastery. In no way does our maturity determine our value, but it does determine the level of responsibility we can handle.

> - **Pursue relationships characterized by love bonds**
> - **Identify tasks of maturity that need work**
> - **Identify past wounds and seek help for healing**
>   *Life Model* page 58

THE INFANT STAGE
Ideal Age: Birth > Age 4

Needs
Joy bonds with both parents that are strong, loving, caring, secure
Important needs are met without asking
Quiet together time
Help regulating distressing emotions
Be seen through the "eyes of heaven"
Receive and give life
Have others synchronize with him/her first

Tasks
Receive with joy
Learn to synchronize with others
Organize self into a person through imitation
Learn to regulate emotions
Learn to return to joy from every emotion
Learn to be the same person over time
Learn self-care skills
Learn to rest

THE CHILD STAGE
Ideal Age: Ages 4 > 13

Needs
- Weaning
- Help to do what he does not feel like doing
- Help sorting feelings, imaginations and reality
- Feedback on guesses, attempts and failures
- Be taught the family history
- Be taught the history of God's family
- Be taught the "big picture" of life

Tasks
- Take care of self (one is enough right now)
- Learn to ask for what he/she needs
- Learn self-expression
- Develop personal resources and talents
- Learn to make himself/herself understandable to others
- Learn to do hard things
- Learn what satisfies
- Tame the nucleus accumbens – our cravings
- See self through the "eyes of heaven"

THE ADULT STAGE
Ideal Age: Age 13 > first child

Needs
- A rite of passage
- Time to bond with peers and form a group identity
- Inclusion by the same-sex community
- Observing the same sex using their power fairly
- Being given important tasks by his/her community
- Guidance for the personal imprint they will make on history
- Opportunities to share life in partnership

THE ADULT STAGE (Continued)

Tasks
   Take care of two or more at the same time
   Discover the main characteristics of his/her heart
   Proclaim and defend personal and community (group) identity
   Bring self and others back to joy simultaneously
   Develop a personal style that reflects his/her heart
   Learn to protect others from himself/herself
   Learn to diversify and blend roles
   Life-giving sexuality
   Mutual satisfaction in a relationship
   Partnership
   To see others through the "eyes of heaven"

THE PARENT STAGE
Ideal Age: From first child until youngest child becomes an adult at 13

Needs
   To give life
   An encouraging partner
   Guidance from elders
   Peer review from other fathers or mothers
   A secure and orderly environment

Tasks
   Giving without needing to receive in return
   Building a home
   Protecting his/her family
   Serving his/her family
   Enjoying his/her family
   Helping his/her children reach maturity
   Synchronizing with the developing needs of: children, spouse, family, work, & church
   See his/her own children through the "eyes of heaven"

THE ELDER STAGE
Ideal Age: Youngest child is an adult

Needs
A community to call his/her own
Recognition by his/her community
A proper place in the community structure
Have others trust them
Be valued and protected by their community

Tasks
Hospitality
Giving life to those without families
Parent and mature his/her community
Build and maintain a community identity
Act like himself/herself in the midst of difficulty
Enjoy what God puts in each person in the community
    (Seeing each of them through 'eyes of heaven')
Building the trust of others through the elder's own transparency and spontaneity

Chapter 3   RECOVERY

> **We are all in recovery.**
> *Life Model* page 59

1. What is being restored or changed during recovery?

2. Give an example of a Type A trauma and what could result from it.

3. Traumas are events or circumstances that diminish who we are because they prove to be too intense for our emotional strength. What sets the limits for our emotional strength?

4. What does "joy" mean as far as our nervous systems are concerned?

> **Recovery must come before destiny can be reached.**
> *Life Model* page 61

Emotional maturity gives us our stability. Stability does not come from avoiding distressing emotions, instead it comes from learning to act like our Jesus-created-selves while we are still emotionally distressed. The Life Model calls this "returning to joy." There are seven major emotions that require a return to joy. (Life Model page 68) All of these paths back to joy are learned by modeling our responses after someone with whom we have a bond. Remember that joy means we are glad to be together—even in our distress and upset emotions.

5. Which of the six major emotions can you feel and still act like a relational person with the same goals and values you have when you feel joy? I know the way back to joy from:
    ___ Shame   ___ Anger   ___ Disgust
    ___ Fear   ___ Sadness   ___ Hopeless/despair

When we know the way back to joy, we will suffer but not be traumatized by our distress—unless it completely exceeds our joy strength. When that happens we lose the capacity to synchronize our brain internally as well as synchronize our needs and feelings with the people around us.

Sometimes we have trouble staying emotionally stable and synchronized both inside and out because we have not received the experience and training we need to return to joy. We can't learn how to get to joy when we are alone. Other times we are simply overwhelmed by emotions that are too strong for our current strength, emotions that exceed our joy strength. Often we must wait until we have grown older and stronger before we can resolve our traumas and learn to suffer without becoming disorganized. This road back we call recovery.

Personal study

1. Beginning with the time before your birth, make a chronological list of your Type A and Type B traumas. Use the Essential Needs And Tasks For Maturity table at the end of Chapter 2 of this study guide to help you figure out your Type A traumas.

    Use additional pages as needed.

Chronology of the A and B traumas in my life

- Events and circumstances that were present before my birth but affected my life.
- Infancy
- Preschool
- Grade school
- Junior High
- High School
- Young adult

Age   **Trauma type**   **Description**

Lies and Wounds

> When we are wounded, we come to wrong conclusions about our selves and our world.
> *Life Model* page 86

Unhealed emotional wounds contain elements that distort our ideas and experience of what "feels true." *Defective explanations* and their right hemispheric twin *incompletely processed painful experiences* can both be helped by exposure to truth. We will first examine how truth in our ideas can be helpful.

This study guide will also introduce the six steps of the Immanuel Process. Starting on the next page the study guide with lead you through the steps that allow God to help you complete your processing of painful events from your past that make distorted beliefs *feel true*. First, let us look at what we normally think of as lies. These could be beliefs like, "I am always going to be a failure."

2. List some of the lies that have kept you "stuck."

3. What help do you need to fight the power of those lies? (Life Model pp.83-84)

4. Name someone in your life who could help you reinforce truth.

5. Read over the four guidelines listed on page 90 of the Life Model.

   a) Which steps have you taken?

   b) What is your next move?

> **Summary**
> 1. **Identify your type A and B traumas.**
> 2. **Identify the emotions where you get stuck and can't get back to joy.**
> 3. **Identify your wounds and lies (deceptions about yourself and your world.)**
> 4. **Let Jesus speak truth to your deceptions in the company of those who pray.**
> *Life Model* page 90

A Six Step Process For Resolving Traumas (Revised from the 8 Step Process)

One characteristic of traumatic memories is that they do not include the awareness of the active and relational presence of the true living Jesus with us. The steps involved in bringing the presence of Jesus to our awareness also serve to resolve the traumatic nature of memories.

While we are aware from scriptural promises that Jesus is always with us (Mt. 28:20), when we are upset, overwhelmed or distracted much of our lives go by without an active awareness of God with us - Immanuel. The Immanuel Approach has been developed and described by Dr. Karl and Charlotte Lehman and more information about it can be found on their website www.kclehman.com. We are grateful for their help in articulating and teaching these steps.

Trauma - the incomplete or improper processing of experience into memory can go wrong at five different levels. While this is not the place to explain those five levels, it is the place to say that awareness of the active presence of Jesus in our memory does resolve trauma at all five levels. While resolving trauma does not end the story or all suffering, it does allow us to go forward with life, acting responsibly like ourselves.

Our experiences with Jesus are attached to memories just as traumatic events are. To help our minds deal with the times when we are not aware of His presence we begin by remembering the times when we were aware of His presence. Asking Jesus to guide us to a specific memory that will help us connect actively with Him often takes us to a memory we might not have thought about, one with some special characteristic needed for our healing this time.

1) Clearly focus on a time when you were aware of the presence of Jesus in your life. Remember the interaction and how it felt to you. For people who have received healing before, these are often memories of how they experienced Jesus at the end of a healed memory.

Note: Do not proceed to any traumatic memories until you have active recall of a good interaction with God. Only then proceed with step 2.

2) From your experience in Jesus' active presence look at a painful/traumatic memory where you are not aware of His presence. At this point things can go three ways:

   a. Jesus takes the lead - If you have a strong connection with Jesus you can simply ask Him what He wants to show you, follow His lead and this will lead you to step 6.

   b. You lead Jesus to where you need Him - Ask Jesus to help you be aware of His presence in the painful memory you want to have healed. If you quickly become aware of Jesus in the memory then go to step 5. If you cannot perceive Jesus' presence in the painful memory go to steps 3 and 4.

   c. Someone needs to lead you to a better connection - If you have difficulty connecting with the painful memory try praying with someone you trust. It sometimes helps to talk about the memory until you feel some connection to the images and emotions. Once you feel connected then ask Jesus to help you be aware of His presence in the painful memory you want to have healed. If you quickly become aware of Jesus in the memory at this point then go to step 5. If you cannot perceive Jesus' presence in the painful memory go to steps 3 and 4.

3) If you cannot perceive Jesus' presence as you examine the painful memory return your focus to the memory where you were experiencing Jesus' presence. Think simultaneously about both memories, the one where you are aware of His presence and the painful memory. From the memory where Jesus is present, talk to Him about the memory where you cannot see Him.

   a. If you do not see Jesus in the painful memory then ask Him to help you see what prevents you from being aware of His presence in the memory of the upsetting experience.

   b. If the traumatic memory causes you to lose and forget all about the memory with the active presence of Jesus then return to the memory of Jesus. If this continues to happen then pray through this process with someone who can help you remember the memory with Jesus present while you think about the traumatic memory. Your prayer partner will need to remind you frequently about the Jesus memory as you ask Him to help you see what keeps you from perceiving His presence in the traumatic time.

   c. It helps to journal or tell someone your thoughts in response to asking Jesus, "What keeps me from perceiving you in this memory?" If necessary, return to your first memory and talk with Jesus about what happens to you and what you think in the traumatic memory.

4) Do what Jesus tells you to clear blockage, which often involves following a memory trail to something that keeps you from perceiving His presence. Sometimes there are decisions and choices you need to make, actions to take or other memories that must be explored first. While following this path come back to the memories where you can remember and interact with Jesus if you reach a spot where you cannot hear or sense a response from God.

5) Interact with the active presence of Jesus in the painful memory. When you reach the point where you perceive Jesus in the traumatic memory, take time to interact with Him until you reach the place where you are resting and enjoying each other. Sometimes this will mean that Jesus tells you He wants you to look at something else first but most often, we tend to push ahead to other thoughts too soon and leave unresolved issues and miss the recharge of joy and peace we need after the healing.

6) You give thanks. Take time to experience a deep feeling of appreciation. This is good for resetting your nervous system to normal and God likes it too.

Sometimes the nature of our painful memories directly hinge on the feeling that God is not there for us and we are unable to perceive His presence at almost any place in our lives. For these kinds of trauma memories Karl and Charlotte have developed Immanuel Interventions that restore the capacity to perceive Jesus' presence in the first place. Those who require this additional step are advised to consult the Lehman's work at www.kclehman.com and view their series of videos on the Immanuel Interventions for the solution to a total inability to perceive Jesus' presence.

Group discussion questions

1. How does the concept of recovery fit in with the big picture of salvation?

2. What are you aware of in your life that you know needs God's healing?

3. How has God been a part of your recovery process?

> **When the time comes to devote our lives to reaching our destiny, we must be properly prepared.**
> *Life Model* page 61

4. How has the community and God's family been a part of your recovery process?

5. When have you been aware of experiencing joy?

6. What experiences, memories or dreams help you picture 'Joy Camp'?

7. Who is in your 'camping group', who will notice if you are 'lost', and will gladly help you back to peace?

8. How long does it take for you to return to joy from fear, shame, hopelessness, guilt, sadness, and anger?

Trauma and old wounds

There are four stages to healing old wounds:

9. Which of the four stages is the most difficult for you?

> 1. **Recognizing the extent and severity of the wound.**
> 2. **Facing the pain.**
> 3. **Receiving the healing that God has for you.**
> 4. **Welcoming new life-giving relationships to help you on the path of maturity.**

10. Which of the type A and B wounds are harder for you to recognize?

11. What happens to someone's identity when they are in pain from an old wound?

12. What happens to someone's identity when an old wound is healed?

13. What are common distortions (lies) about themselves or the world that affect people with old wounds?

14. How has God freed you from some of the lies you have believed in the past?

15. What has happened to your identity when you had lies removed or wounds healed?

16. What is the most effective way to remove lies about our identities and the world?

Chapter 4   BELONGING

> The family of God is made up of the people God brings into your life who give you what your heart needs.
> *Life Model* page 94

1. What is "belonging?"

2. Why does "belonging" matter?

3. What are the two ways in which we can belong to a family?

Jesus' teaching on spiritual adoption

What did Jesus teach and practice about spiritual adoption? We can find out from studying the Gospel of John. If spiritual family was central to the teachings and life of Jesus, as we believe it was, then we will find this spiritual family is necessary for living the way He wants us to live.

Family is the source of our life—or is it? John raises this issue immediately in his Gospel. "All that came to be was alive with his life" John said of Jesus. (John 1:4 NEB) Next he addresses how we become a family member in the family that is alive. John says that those who yield Jesus their allegiance—we would say "bond"—he gives the power to "become the offspring of God himself." (John 1:13 NEB) This, John says, is better than becoming family because your parents were having pleasure. Jesus, as the only true child of God, has the right to give us rights as family members too. (John 1:14) We are all adopted if we are to be alive.

Spiritual adoption went directly against Jewish thought that held that having a Jewish mother made you a part of God's chosen family. The conflict surfaced early in John's story as Jesus told Nicodemus that his first birth did not make him alive and a second was needed—this time by the Spirit. Nicky naturally thought his mother should be involved but Jesus was insistent on a spiritual adoption. Jesus again claimed to be the only legitimate member of God's family. (John 3:16)

No sooner did Jesus say his family brings you closer to God than a Jewish mother could, but he went to the other branch of the biological family (the Samaritans in chapter 4) and declared himself greater than their ancestor Jacob. Again he insisted that they join God's family by asking him for life, water and food. He proclaimed life and worship in the spirit—spiritual adoption. (John 4:23) Having the "wrong" biological family made no difference if one wanted to be a child of God.

From beginning to end, Jesus fought with Jewish leaders over who was a legitimate family member in God's family. The Jews trusted their biology. Jesus said that the biological family was a killer family that went back to the Devil. (John 8:44) Even his own biological family could not qualify as members of God's family without believing him. (John 7:5) Jesus forced those who did believe in him to choose which family they trusted for life. (John 8:30-59) His opponents forced people to the same choice, as the man born blind and his family found out. (John 9) The man who received his sight lost his family and was banned from the synagogue while his parents chose to stay with their own people and lose both Jesus and their son. So, you now must answer the question too. Which family gives you life and which one kills you? Before you complete the personal study and group discussion, go to the end of this chapter and complete the Bible study on spiritual adoption in the Gospel of John.

Personal study

1. After giving some serious consideration to your spiritual family, who are the people you are sure God has placed in your life?

2. Can you think of someone God brought into your life to help you meet your maturity needs?

3. What is it about that person that made you want to accept them into your life?

4. How would you describe the current quality of your spiritual family relationships?

5. What are the overlaps and conflicts between your spiritual and natural families?

6. Do you want your spiritual family to grow?

7. Will you commit to talk to God and one other person every day this week about what it means to join a spiritual family?

8. What do you currently need from the family of God?

9. Name some people in your community or God's family that could help you with these needs.

10. What do you feel when you think about receiving the things you need for your maturity through someone in a relationship?
    ___ fear   ___ hope
    ___ apprehension   ___ no feeling (Can't imagine it happening)
    ___ doubt   ___ relief

11. If you thought it was possible, what type of spiritual adoption would you want to experience? (parent, brother, sister, child, other?)

12. What do you imagine such an adoptive relationship would look like?

13. How will you know whether this is God's plan or your idea?

Group discussion questions

1. What are the ways in which we find out where we really belong?

> In our journey of healing and maturing, we need a family and a community of caring men, women, and friends. Different people will be better equipped than others to meet our varied needs.

2. What are the things we cannot give ourselves and that God will only give us through others?

3. Which is harder for you: to entrust yourself to God directly to meet your needs, or to depend on others within the family of believers?

4. What makes this difficult for you?

5. What feelings or thoughts come up for you when you think of the term "spiritual adoption"?

6. Do any group members need a bigger spiritual family? Make a list of one need from each group member and then ask God to meet those needs.

7. When you think that God might want you to provide part of the family that wounded people need, what reactions do you have?

8. How do you know when people are "rescuing" others and being "co-dependent" and when they are following God's lead in forming spiritual family relationships?

> Wounded people need real, live, loving families. That is what the family of God is supposed to be.
> *Life Model* page 97

9. How well do you join in the church or "community" relationships available for you?

10. Tell the group one thing you will do this week to participate more fully in the opportunities already available for you.

Spiritual Adoption in the Gospel of John

The Struggle Over Who Is God's Family: The Two Families[1]

1. When Jesus entered the world he came to us through God's chosen ones – the Jews, descendants of Abraham. Many believed that this automatically made them children of God. Their spiritual heritage was a given; they were God's family. Jesus disavowed biological heritage as the basis for spiritual status. **What does Jesus claim in John 1:12-13 as the basis for being in God's family?**

2. In fact, Jesus carried this a step further when he told Nicodemus in John 3:3: "I tell you the truth, … no one can enter the kingdom of God unless he is born of water and the Spirit." **Why was this such a shock to Jewish logic about family?**

---
[1] All scripture references from the NIV Study Bible

3. Jesus backed up his words with actions. In John 4 we read of his conversation with the Samaritan woman at the well. We find out in verse 18 that the woman had had 5 husbands and her current man was not her husband. **What does this say about her family?**

4. Jesus broke all the barriers; not only by talking with the woman, accepting a drink from her, but explaining to her how God seeks those who worship him in spirit and in truth. The woman went back to her people telling them she thought she had met "the Christ" (4:29), who knew "everything I ever did". **According to verses 40 and 41, how did Jesus continue to challenge their deeply held belief about who belonged in God's family?**

5. This message, this new definition of how to become family, was not received well by the Jews. **Which people are examined as the possible sources of God's spiritual family in John 7:19-22, 28-31 and 8:37-47?**

6. While Jesus and his disciples were fleeing from being stoned for his statements about spiritual family, they came across a man who had been born blind. Jesus took this opportunity to reveal the man's heart while healing his eyes. Later the man's neighbors, perplexed and baffled by his sudden healing, brought him to the Pharisees. The man explained in John 9:15 how Jesus had healed him. **Based on the Pharisee's response in verse 16, how did they disqualify Jesus from belonging in God's family?**

7. The Pharisees then sent for the man's parents. **What do verses 18-23 tell us about this man's biological (and supposedly spiritual) family?**

8. Left on his own, he argued with the Pharisees over which family Jesus came from, and held his own with these powerful men. The leaders made it clear that anyone who believed Jesus was not part of their spiritual family at the synagogue. **When Jesus removes the veil from your eyes so you can see Him, to whom do you go to tell the story?**

The Character of Family Life in God's Family

We have looked at the kind of family that destroys, does not give life. What does it mean to be part of Jesus' family—the family of God? Jesus set an example of being the life-giver.

1. Jesus sought out the lonely and abandoned. Just as he drew the Samaritan woman into a conversation, gently revealing her need for a Savior, he also sought out the man he had healed of blindness. **After hearing that he had been cast out of the synagogue, Jesus went to look for him (9:35). What conflicts had resulted from his healing?**

2. Jesus spent time with those he was personally investing in. During his short time on earth, Jesus spoke to thousands of people. At the same time he drew out 12 men, calling them to follow him. **After looking at John 1:35-39, 2:12, 3:22, 6:3, 9:2, and 11:54 what words would you use to describe Jesus' relationship to his disciples?**

3. Look again at John's account in 6:1-13 of the feeding of the five thousand. **What do verses 5 and 6 tell us about how Jesus tried to involve the disciples in the miracle?**

4. Jesus prayed for them (17:6-19). Some have referred to John 17 as the "love chapter." **What do Jesus' words in 17:6 show about his commitment to his spiritual family?**

5. Jesus poured his life into these men showing them his Father's heart. He loved each one and yet John refers to himself as "the disciple whom Jesus loved." **What does the passage in John 13:21 – 25 tell us about the kind of bond they shared?**

6. Jesus showed his trust in John just before he died, while hanging on the cross. **In John 19:26-27 how did Jesus bring his spiritual and biological family together?**

Jesus didn't need the same intimate relationship with the other disciples in order to apprentice them. Neither is it necessary for us to be intimately connected with every member of our church. God gave John to Jesus because God knew what a blessing it would be for his Son. If God knew how much even Jesus needed this love, how much more do we need to experience life-giving relationships as well!

Community Support Checklist
Personal prayer support for people in life change or counseling:

List five people who are praying for your growth and recovery. These people should be updated on your progress and needs each week.

1. _____ 2. _____

3. _____ 4. _____

5. _____

The care of your soul:

Please list the two people who take personal responsibility for the care of your soul as though you were their own child. Who sees to it that you are prospering in your growth and are not hurt in your relationship to God and others?

Spiritual Mother: _____

Spiritual Father: _____

Others: _____

Your sources for prayer and ministry:

Where do you receive your corrective and restorative prayer ministry for each of the following?

Healing: Group: _____

Contact person: _____ phone: _____

Deliverance/spiritual warfare: Group: _____

Contact person: _____ phone: _____

Fellowship: Group: _____

Contact person: _____ phone: _____

Permission granted to copy this page.

Chapter 5 YOUR HEART

True knowing and false knowing

Although this is the simplest idea in the LIFE Model, knowing what is good is the hardest part of the LIFE model to understand—for most of us. It requires us to wear our brain at a different angle than we usually do, so to speak. Unless we are distressed about our own efforts to do what is right, we miss the simple and obvious—yet unbelievable—answer.

1. According to this chapter of the Life Model, what are the two ways of knowing "the right thing to do?"

2. "No human can correctly distinguish good from evil." (Life Model page 109) How does this differ from what you have thought or been taught?

Acting like yourself

People often express they don't know what identity they received through the heart that Jesus gave them. For many it is difficult to grasp the concept that somewhere they contain a true person, created by God. It might help to use our imaginations and go back to a time before time. There was a celebration going on in heaven. Angels were a-buzz with wonder and delight! God loved people and wanted to create lots of them but keep them all unique! Each one different from the other billions of unique blends and yet each made in God's image. God blended tailor-made traits to match His life-giving plans for each one's life. The creativity flowed; a double dose of wisdom and kindness for one, gloriously abundant truth and justice given to another. This one was taller, that one sang like a bird and another one was fueled with extra strong mercy and compassion. God's works were magnificent! Every one was shining with glories. Each special work hidden at first but ready to be revealed on earth (in some small package) at just the right time. God stepped back exclaiming, "It is good!" Then, God rested with joy.

3. What does Ephesians 2:10 tell us we will do if we act like ourselves—what we are calling living from the heart Jesus gave us?

4. In John 9:3 Jesus uses the same word for works we just saw in Ephesians 2:10. Here Jesus tells his disciples that a man was born blind so that "God's works in him might be revealed." Just like Jesus did in the story we call "the widow's mite" (Mark 12:41-44) where he pointed out who really gave the most to God, Jesus now points out who in town can really see. What were the "works of God" in the man people thought was blind from birth? Asked another way, what hidden identity did God have in the man people saw as blind?

5. Do you think the blind man knew what works were hidden in him by God before Jesus stopped to put mud in his eyes? Asked another way, was he as surprised as the rest about what it meant to act like himself?

Personal study

1. What are some of your greatest passions in life?

> One sign that you have found the characteristics of your heart is when your passion, purposes, talents and pain all come together and begin defining who you are.
> *Life Model* page 113

2. What characteristics of your heart relate to each of your passions?

3. When do your true passions cause you to suffer? (An example would be someone who loves children sees pictures from a famine where children are starving.)

4. What have you learned about your heart from the things that you have suffered?

5. How could your pain combine with your passion and talents to define who you are?

6. What do you see as the main characteristic of your heart?

7. When have you used the sark as your guide?

8. How do you tell the difference between guidance from your heart and your sark?

9. When are you most tempted to prove you are doing the right thing?

10. What situation in your current life have you been "sticking to your guns" because you are sure that you are right?

11. Does your heart find joy in the stand you are taking about being right?

12. Would you spend intentional time looking to God, insuring that your perspective matches His?

Note: *After answering these questions in your own personal study, think about sharing some of them with the group. What would it take for you to feel comfortable sharing your heart with your group at this level?*

If you have trouble recognizing your heart

1. If you have trouble recognizing your heart, who would know you well enough to help you see when you are acting like yourself?

2. Make a commitment to meet with that person to ask them to tell you about your heart. Allow at least one hour.

    Date _____.

3. Ask God to show you your heart. Allow at least an hour.

    Date _____.

> "Through our hearts we see ourselves as God sees us."
> *Life Model* page 113

4. What feelings come up for you when you think of God showing you your heart?

5. How do you think your closest friend (or whoever it is that you think knows you best) would describe you?

6. Would you tell your best friend the main characteristic of his heart?

Group discussion questions

1. How would you describe the sark (false knowing) in your own words?

> We do things the way we do because we believe our way will 'work' and 'be right'. Yet scripture tells us not to use our own understanding, but to discern God in all our ways. That way He will direct us.

2. How can you tell when the sark is present and active? What are its characteristic effects?

3. Why is the sark always wrong?

4. How does true knowing (living out of your heart) contrast to the sark?

5. Do you know when you are acting like yourself?

6. How do you feel when you do something out of your heart?

7. Give an example of a time when you were authentically or spontaneously yourself and did something right from your heart that brought you joy.

8. What is the difference between acting on your feelings and living out of your heart?

Heart Characteristics

1. What feelings come up for you when you think of God seeing your heart?

> **Living from the heart Jesus gave you means you are being the person you were designed to be. You are acting like yourself.**
> *Life Model* page 113

2. What is life like when we lose track of the true characteristics of our hearts?

3. Have you recognized unique heart traits in other members of our group?

4. What are some of the characteristics of your heart?

5. Who has helped see you through God's eyes and told you about your heart?

6. Do you know anyone outside the group who has lost track of their hearts?

7. Can you tell them one of the lost characteristics?

Chapter 6   LIVING THE LIFE MODEL

Write a short analysis of your church (current or past) according to LIFE Model principles. What are your church's strengths and weaknesses in relationship to maturity, recovery, belonging, joy and living from your hearts?

Personal study

1. Who have been your examples because of the way they lived LIFE Model principles?

2. Name three people who are a source of life for you. After each name indicate how you can increase his or her joy this week.

   1) _____

   Joy plan:

   2) _____

   Joy plan:

   3) _____

   Joy plan:

3. Name three people who receive life from you. After each name indicate how you can increase his or her joy this week.

   1) _____

   Joy plan:

   2) _____

   Joy plan:

   3) _____

   Joy plan:

Group Discussion Questions

1. Who in your church and family has reached real elder maturity?

2. What is one trusting step you (or your study group) can take to build on their maturity?

3. What is your pastor's maturity level?

4. How should your pastor's job expectations be changed to take maturity into account?

5. If you do not know your pastor's maturity level, what would happen if you asked?

6. What is the highest maturity level your pastor could have achieved by now?

7. What is the maturity level of the missionaries that your church supports, and how should that reflect in their assignments?

8. What do you, your family or your church do when:
   1) A boy or girl reaches 13?

   2) A man or woman has their first child?

9. What would it take to improve what is being done to promote maturity by:
   1) You

   2) Your family

3) Your church

4) What would be the smallest change you could make?

> - **Church leaders have reached at least an adult level of maturity**
> - **Recognition of the effects of trauma on maturity**
> - **Care in selecting leaders who are mature**
> - **Recognition of the power of redemption in people's lives**
> - **Led by the Holy Spirit into redemptive works**
> - **An understanding of the importance of joy in human growth**
> - **Encouraging marriage only between people of adult maturity**
> - **Actively encourage and aid parents in cherishing their children**

10. Characteristics of a church community that lives by the LIFE Model are listed on pages 127-131 of the book. Which characteristics have you seen evidence of in your church communities?

11. Which ones seem to be missing from your present church community?

12. Do the spiritual families in your church seem to grow under the conviction that they are being formed by God or according to what strikes people as a good plan?

13. What have been the three most upsetting events in the life of your church?

    a. _____

    b. _____

    c. _____

14. How does your church return to joy after something upsetting has happened?

15. Who are the wounded in your church?

16. Do you want more wounded people in your church?

17. Who will admit to being wounded in your church or family?

18. How long do the wounded have to get better?

19. What treatment is given to the wounded at your church or family?

20. How do the wounded bring life to your family and church?

Closing time

We suggest that your group consider one or more of the following activities as a closing time for your group study.

- Have a meal together.
- Each group member gives the other members some simple object that symbolizes an important aspect of that person's heart.
- Each group member call, write, e-mail, or invite out one person. Tell him or her what you have learned that changed your life or gave you joy.

Additional Life Model Resources

No	Sometimes	Usually	Always	**Infant stage** **Motivations and Regulations**
				I have experienced strong, loving, caring bonds with mother/a women.
				I have experienced strong, loving, caring bonds with father/a man.
				Important needs were met until I learned to ask.
				Others took the lead and synchronized with me and my feelings first.
				Quiet together times helped me calm myself with people around.
				Important people have seen me through the "eyes of heaven."
				I can both receive and give life.
				I receive with joy and without guilt or shame.
				I can now synchronize with others and their feelings.
				I found people to imitate so that I now have a personality I like.
				I learned to regulate and quiet the "big six" emotions:
				Anger
				Fear
				Sadness
				Disgust
				Shame
				hopeless/despair
				I can return to joy from every emotion and restore broken relationships.
				I stay the same person over time.
				I know how to rest.

From *Living With Men* by Jim Wilder arranged by Ken Smith

No	Sometimes	Usually	Always	**Child stage** **Competency**
				I can do things I don't feel like doing.
				I can do hard things (even if they cause me some pain.)
				I can separate my feelings, my imagination and reality in my relationships.
				I am comfortable with reasonable risks, attempts and failures.
				I have received love I did not have to earn.
				I know how my family came to be the way it is--family history.
				I know how God's family came to be the way it is.
				I know the "big picture" of life with the stages of maturity.
				I can take care of myself.
				I ask for for what I need.
				I enjoy self-expression.
				I am growing in the things I am good at doing (personal resources and talents.)
				I help other people to understand me better if they don't respond well to me.
				I have learned to control my cravings.
				I know what satisfies me.
				I see myself through the "eyes of heaven."

No	Sometimes	Usually	Always	**Adult stage**
				I have had a rite of passage into adulthood by the community
				I am comfortable relating to the same sex community
				I have a peer group where I belong
				I can partner with others
				My relationships are marked by fairness and mutual satisfaction
				I protect others from my power when necessary
				I protect my personal and group identity when boundaries are violated
				I live in a way that expresses my heart
				I have a diverse set of roles and responsibilities
				I make important contributions to my family and community
				I can bring two or more people back to joy at the same time
				I use my sexual power wisely
				I can proclaim my spiritual identity
				I can see others through the "eyes of Heaven."

From *Living With Men* by Jim Wilder arranged by Ken Smith

No	Sometimes	Usually	Always	**Pre-marriage Check List for Men**
				I have a well developed adult maturity
				My labors are productive
				I give life to others with style
				I have experienced life as:
				Brother
				Friend
				Priest
				Lover
				Warrior
				King
				Servant
				All of these together

No	Sometimes	Usually	Always	**Parent Stage**
				I have brought others to life
				I have an encouraging partner
				I receive guidance from elders
				I have peers that hold me accountable
				I have a secure and orderly home and community
				I can give without needing to receive in return
				I see my family through the eyes of heaven
				I include others in family activities
				I am present with my family
				I am protective of my family
				I am attentive to my family
				I am calming to my family
				I enjoy my family
				I comfort my family
				I help my children mature
				I can synchronize the needs of wife, children, family, work & church

From *Living With Men* by Jim Wilder arranged by Ken Smith

No	Sometimes	Usually	Always	**Elder Stage**
				I have a community of people to call my own
				I am recognized by my community
				I have a proper place in the community structure
				I am valued and defended by the community
				I demonstrate hospitality
				I give life to the "familyless"
				I help my community mature
				I build and maintain the community identity
				I don't abandon when I disengage
				I share others' feelings but still know who I am and who they are
				I continue to be the same person when provoked or tempted
				I bear up well under:
				Misunderstandings
				Accusations
				Rage
				Contradictions
				I see some of what God sees in every situation
				I enjoy what God put in each and everyone
				I live transparently and spontaneously
				I build and rebuild trust

The LIFE Model of Redemption and Maturity

So hurt people wouldn't spend their lives simply recovering and "getting by," a small but dedicated group of pastors, counselors, prayer ministers, deliverance workers, abuse survivors, support people and parents looked, studied and prayed their way to a model that would guide us from birth to death—a LIFE model.

A growing number of books, tapes, videos, conferences and training seminars use aspects of the life model but its essentials are found in a small book called The Life Model: Living From The Heart Jesus Gave You. This book has been translated in several languages. The LIFE Model is used around the world for trauma treatment, addiction recovery, community development, church design, child rearing and Christian missions.

The LIFE Model is, as its name implies, a model for life from conception to death. It is an idealized model, that is to say, it proposes what life should be like rather than describing what life on earth generally produces. The LIFE model suggests that people need five things in order to thrive:

1. A place to belong
2. To receive and give life
3. The capacity to recover from things that go wrong (desynchronizations)
4. To mature as they get older
5. To live from their identities (hearts)

These elements develop when we share joy and sorrows together as natural and spiritual families in peaceful homes. The LIFE Model covers both our growth and recovery. These five elements apply whether we consider physical growth, emotional growth, family growth, community growth or spiritual growth. Taken in order from one to five, these elements are needed for strong and healthy human growth. Taken in reverse order, starting with living from our true identities, these same elements form an excellent diagnostic grid for a failure to thrive.

By understanding the causes for failures to thrive we can design a restoration process. The LIFE Model explains how to restore our identities as individuals, families and communities so that we live from a completely synchronized and authentic identity we call "the heart that Jesus gives us." This authentic identity is as much communal as it is individual.

Deep in the right hemisphere of every human brain is a control center that develops during the first two years after conception. This center will run our lives and bodies and, provided we develop a strong one, will see us through the tempests of life. We seek to train and restore this control center. With it we can regulate our emotions, act like ourselves and stay synchronized inside and out.

We become traumatized when the emotional intensity of life exceeds our capacity to maintain synchronization between the four levels of our control center. Thriving means building a strong control center through joyful attachment bonds that bring peace and return us to joy when we become upset.

We develop our identities by responding and resonating when we see the characteristics we possess expressed by an older and more experienced person. Identity is propagated like cuttings from live plants and not grown from seeds. This way of growing an identity by receiving the life passed on from one who went before is true for us at a physical level just as it is at an emotional and spiritual level.

What makes the LIFE Model a Christian model is a division between redemption and maturity. While most people will agree that not everyone matures correctly, some would say that all human beings could reach their full maturity by purely human means. Christians would say, "not without help." Some believe that everything needed for full human maturity is already contained within each person. Christians would say, "Something is still missing."

It takes a mutual effort between people and their God to fully live and experience life as it was meant to be lived. God clearly separates divine areas of responsibility from human areas of responsibility. Humans are responsible for maturity. God is responsible for redemption.

The LIFE Model is a profoundly Christian blueprint for wholeness for individuals, families, churches and communities across the lifespan.

The LIFE Model is a unifying approach to ministries of counseling, recovery, pastoral care, prayer ministry, deliverance, inner healing, child rearing, body life and health.

The LIFE Model is used internationally for substance abuse recovery programs. It has been widely used as a church model. Missions have adopted the model for the restoration of missionary children. Almost every major ministry that deals with trauma and abuse victims in the USA uses and distributes the LIFE Model as part of their teaching.

The theory behind this book was developed at Shepherd's House Inc. in California. Pastors, counselors, prayer team members, lay leaders, people in recovery and an international advisory panel from many traditions and theoretical perspectives worked together to formulate this profoundly Christian view of life.

Where can I learn more about the Life Model?

www.lifemodel.org

Overview of the Life Model, downloads, handouts, resources in various languages, materials for sale, training, staff, events, contact information, newsletters, projects, donations, Shepherd's House Inc., current board membership and not-for-profit corporate information, maps of Life Model activities and a central search function can be located at this web site.

www.thrivetoday.org

THRIVE is intensive skill training for your nervous system and spirit. THRIVE is a brilliant and complete training program using brain science and the presence of Jesus to free you from fears and struggles that waste so much life. Down inside, you have always known there was something more to friendship, parenting, marriage, church or even counseling, than what you have seen. You have worked hard, tried the usual spiritual and counseling solutions but didn't thrive. THRIVE is the strategic solution for the training you missed growing up! With THRIVE you increase your capacity to handle distressing emotions and stay productive. The joy-people at Shepherd's House designed THRIVE for you, using the Life Model.

THRIVE applies the Life Model's 19 brain and character skills. THRIVE makes joy your foundation - spiritually, mentally and relationally. THRIVE lets you feel loved while you master difficult emotions. THRIVE helps you live in God's presence so you are transformed. THRIVE helps you stay connected with the people you love - even in painful emotions! THRIVE training includes international conferences, maturity retreats where you live or training materials you can use at home.

www.thrivingrecovery.org

Thriving: Recover Your Life is an innovative and comprehensive life training program comprised of 5 different modules that will help you:

- Learn skills to engage God in order to grow spiritually
- Recover from painful addictions, trauma and attachment pain
- Learn to create community and healthy relationships around you
- Discover how to experience the presence of God in a way that heals
- Experience how God can heal the barriers that we put up in our relationships

One of the most unique and exciting elements of Thriving: Recover Your Life is that it brings people of all levels of maturity together to build a joyful healing community. This is one aspect of our program that you won't find anywhere else. Participants heal and grow by building joy in the context of secure, healthy relationships with God and others. As joy builds, they are better able to handle distress and increasingly able to live from their heart.

Thriving: Recover Your Life incorporates the latest advances in neuroscience with the Life Model concepts and the 19 relationship skills needed to thrive. This program is revolutionizing churches, recovery programs and other ministries all over the world.